British Library Cataloguing in Publication Data

The Twelve days of Christmas.—(Square books)
   1. Carols, English—Text
   I. Langton, Roger
   783.6'52    PR1195.C2
   ISBN 0-7214-9580-X

First edition

Published by Ladybird Books Ltd Loughborough Leicestershire UK
Ladybird Books Inc Lewiston Maine 04240 USA

Printed in England

# The twelve days of Christmas

illustrated by Roger Langton

Ladybird Books

On the first day of Christmas
my true love sent to me,
a partridge in a pear tree.

On the second day of Christmas
my true love sent to me,
two turtledoves
and a partridge in a pear tree.

On the third day of Christmas
my true love sent to me,
three French hens,
two turtledoves
and a partridge in a pear tree.

On the fourth day of Christmas
my true love sent to me,
four calling birds,
three French hens,
two turtledoves
and a partridge in a pear tree.

On the fifth day of Christmas
my true love sent to me,
five gold rings,
four calling birds,
three French hens,
two turtledoves
and a partridge in a pear tree.

On the sixth day of Christmas
my true love sent to me,
six geese a-laying,
five gold rings,
four calling birds,
three French hens,
two turtledoves
and a partridge in a pear tree.

On the seventh day of Christmas
my true love sent to me,
seven swans a-swimming,
six geese a-laying,
five gold rings,
four calling birds,
three French hens,
two turtledoves
and a partridge in a pear tree.

On the eighth day of Christmas
my true love sent to me,
eight maids a-milking,
seven swans a-swimming,
six geese a-laying,
five gold rings,
four calling birds,
three French hens,
two turtledoves
and a partridge in a pear tree.

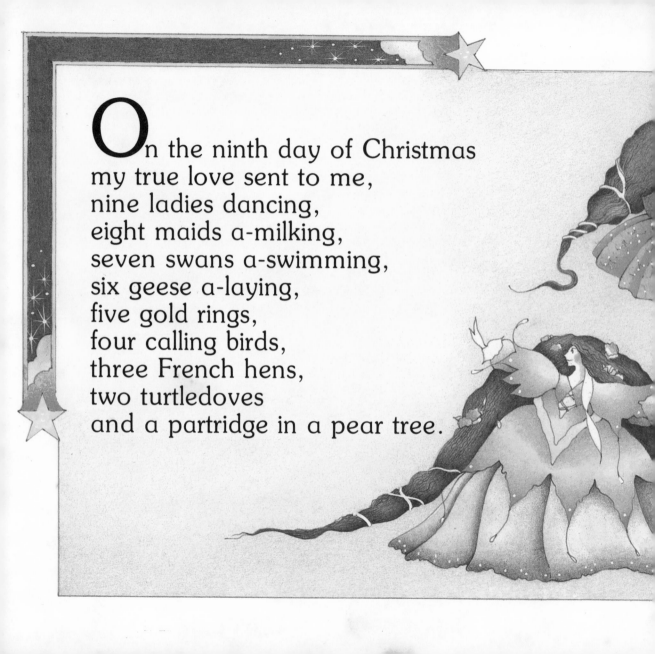

On the ninth day of Christmas
my true love sent to me,
nine ladies dancing,
eight maids a-milking,
seven swans a-swimming,
six geese a-laying,
five gold rings,
four calling birds,
three French hens,
two turtledoves
and a partridge in a pear tree.

On the tenth day of Christmas
my true love sent to me,
ten lords a-leaping,
nine ladies dancing,
eight maids a-milking,
seven swans a-swimming,
six geese a-laying,
five gold rings,
four calling birds,
three French hens,
two turtledoves
and a partridge in a pear tree.

On the eleventh day of Christmas
my true love sent to me,
eleven pipers piping,
ten lords a-leaping,
nine ladies dancing,
eight maids a-milking,
seven swans a-swimming,
six geese a-laying,
five gold rings,
four calling birds,
three French hens,
two turtledoves
and a partridge in a pear tree.

On the twelfth day of Christmas
my true love sent to me,
twelve drummers drumming,
eleven pipers piping,
ten lords a-leaping,
nine ladies dancing,
eight maids a-milking,
seven swans a-swimming,
six geese a-laying,
five gold rings,
four calling birds,
three French hens,
two turtledoves
and a partridge in a pear tree.